Break a Leg!

I dedicate this book to everyone learning a new language and to all who have graciously supported language learners.

Mirella Utsler

© 2024 Mirella Utsler
All rights reserved.
No part of this book may be reproduced in any form without written permission from the author.

This book belongs to:

....

A year ago, the Torres family moved to the United States from South America. Gloria and Ruben were the parents of two amazing kids: Pedro, a 12-year-old, and Sara, a 9-year-old. They were excited about their new life in America and confident about their English skills, having learned the language in Peru, their home country.

Unfortunately, what they experienced was far from what they expected. It seemed like everyone spoke too fast, and when they talked in English, people didn't seem to understand them. Their frustration grew over time, and the cherry on top was an event at the children's school.

It was a special day. Every class had to prepare an act for the talent show. Gloria and Ruben were excited to see the kids perform, but they didn't know that it would be a challenging day for each member of the family.

When the talent show started, the school was full of students and their families. Sara, who was going to sing a song, was getting ready when an old lady smiled and told her, "Break a leg!"

Sara and her family were confused, and Pedro asked, "Why does that lady want Sara to break her leg?"

Sara said, "I don't want to break my leg!"

But their mother added, "I'm sure she said something else."

Luckily, Pedro's friend, Bill, was sitting next to them, and he explained, "No, she's being nice. *Break a leg* means good luck!"

The Torres family was surprised. "Really?" they laughed.

When it was time for Pedro and his team to perform a magic act, his friend, Tim, told him, "This is going to be a piece of cake!" Pedro was confused and gave him a nervous smile. The team did a great job, and the crowd cheered for their outstanding performance.

Afterward, Pedro asked Tim, "And the cake?"
Tim responded, "What cake?"
Bill, who was also on the magic team, said, "Pedro, Tim meant that the magic act was going to be easy."
"So, there's no cake?" asked Pedro.
"No, no cake!" said Bill. Pedro felt so disappointed about not having cake, but the worst part was that he felt dumb.

After the show, all the parents and students sat at the tables in the dining area on the patio, eating and chatting.

Suddenly, another student's mother said, "Let's break the ice!"

Gloria responded, "There's no need; we have ice cubes in the fridge!" Everyone looked at Gloria, and an uncomfortable silence followed until one of the parents laughed. Then, everyone started laughing and talking to each other.

17

Bill was sitting next to Pedro. John, Bill's dad, said, "That was a great icebreaker, Gloria!" She smiled nervously, but she was still confused. She looked to her family for help, but they were confused too. Bill noticed their confusion and explained, "*Break the ice* is what you did, Mrs. Torres. You said something that helped people feel comfortable at the party."

Gloria said, "I'm so confused!" While she was glad she made the other parents comfortable, she felt very frustrated.

John mentioned his birthday was coming up, so Ruben asked, "Any plans for your birthday?"

John said, "I've been putting a bug in my wife's ears for days, but I still don't think she sees that I want to go to the beach for my birthday."

"Are you kidding? Doesn't she get mad?" Ruben asked in shock.

Bill chimed in and said, "Mr. Ruben, my dad meant that he gave my mom a hint of what he wants for his birthday."

Blushing, Ruben said, "Oh! I see!" Although he smiled nervously, he felt dumb.

The event was over, and it was time to clean up. John asked the kids, "Can you give me a hand?" All the kids started picking up except for Pedro and Sara.

I don't think they heard me... thought John. He asked Sara and Pedro, "Can you give me a hand?" The two kids extended their hands out to him.

John smiled, understanding what had just happened, and explained to them, "*Give me a hand* means to please help me." Both kids were embarrassed and started picking up quietly.

It was getting dark and had started raining, so everyone had to get inside.

"It's raining cats and dogs!" said one parent.

Sara whispered to her parents, "No, it's not!"

Gloria said, "I think he meant that it's raining a lot!"

Bill, who heard the conversation, confirmed, "Yes, Mrs. Torres. That's exactly what it means!"

Sara asked, "Why do people speak like this here?"

Gloria explained that they also had these types of expressions in Spanish.

It was time to go, and one person said, "I'm pooped!" Pedro and his family looked at each other and started laughing.

Gloria whispered, "I'm sure it doesn't mean what you all are thinking!" Every member of Pedro's family looked at Bill, who couldn't explain because he was cracking up.

That night, after all the frustration and confusion, the Torres family was tired of feeling dumb. They decided to continue studying English to stop the confusion.

Months later, they were speaking and understanding better than ever, and they couldn't wait to learn even more!

Let's discuss the book.

1. Before reading the book, take a look at its cover. What do you think the book is about, and why?
2. Look at the illustrations. What themes do you think the story will explore?
3. Why does Pedro feel dumb?
4. Why is Mrs. Torres confused?
5. What do you think Ruben understood when John said, "I've been putting a bug in my wife's ears for days"?
6. Can you relate any part of the story to your life? Please share an example.
7. If you could rename the story, what title would you choose and why?
8. Can you identify a cause and effect in the story? How does it enrich the plot?
9. What messages or lessons do you think the story conveys?

www.ingramcontent.com/pod-product-compliance
Lightning Source LLC
Chambersburg PA
CBHW041540040426
42446CB00002B/167